PRICKLY ANIMALS

by Nadia Higgins

pogo

Ideas for Parents and Teachers

Pogo Books let children practice reading informational text while introducing them to nonfiction features such as headings, labels, sidebars, maps, and diagrams, as well as a table of contents, glossary, and index.

Carefully leveled text with a strong photo match offers early fluent readers the support they need to succeed.

Before Reading

- "Walk" through the book and point out the various nonfiction features. Ask the student what purpose each feature serves.
- Look at the glossary together. Read and discuss the words.

Read the Book

- Have the child read the book independently.
- Invite him or her to list questions that arise from reading.

After Reading

- Discuss the child's questions. Talk about how he or she might find answers to those questions.
- Prompt the child to think more. Ask: Have you seen any of the prickly animals mentioned in the book? Can you think of any prickly animals that aren't discussed?

Pogo Books are published by Jump!
5357 Penn Avenue South
Minneapolis, MN 55419
www.jumplibrary.com

Library of Congress Cataloging-in-Publication Data

Higgins, Nadia, author.
  Prickly animals / by Nadia Higgins.
     pages cm. – (Back off! Animal defenses)
  Audience: Ages 7-10.
  Summary: "Carefully leveled text and vibrant photographs introduce readers to prickly animals such as the sea urchin, hedgehog, porcupine, and thorny devil, and explore how they use spines to defend themselves against predators. Includes activity, glossary, and index."–Provided by publisher.
  Includes index.
  ISBN 978-1-62031-311-4 (hardcover: alk. paper) –
  ISBN 978-1-62496-377-3 (ebook)
  1. Animal defenses–Juvenile literature.
  2. Animal weapons–Juvenile literature.
  3. Adaptation (Biology)–Juvenile literature. I. Title.
  QL759.H445 2016
  591.47–dc23
                                    2015032607

Series Editor: Jenny Fretland VanVoorst
Series Designer: Anna Peterson
Book Designer: Ellen Schofield
Photo Researcher: Jenny Fretland VanVoorst

Photo Credits: All photos by Shutterstock except: Getty, 16-17; Science Source Images, 20-21, 23; SuperStock, 5, 11, 14-15; Thinkstock, 18.

Printed in the United States of America at Corporate Graphics in North Mankato, Minnesota.

TABLE OF CONTENTS

CHAPTER 1

DON'T EAT ME!

A sea urchin creeps along the ocean floor. You can barely tell this spiky ball is moving.

Along comes a crab. It is looking for **prey**. What can the sea urchin do? It cannot run away. With luck, its **spines** will keep it safe. The crab will find an easier meal.

For most animals, their prickles are like signs. The signs say, "Don't eat me!"

A sleeping hedgehog curls into a ball. The spines on its back keep most enemies away.

A thorny devil looks about as tasty as a pile of tacks. Its strange skin tells hungry birds to fly on by.

The spiny bump on its neck is a trick head. When danger comes, the lizard hides its real head. A **predator** will attack the bump instead. Maybe the lizard still has a chance.

CHAPTER 2

SHARP WEAPONS

A porcupine's tail is filled with **quills** as sharp as needles. These quills just might save its life.

On the African plains, a porcupine fights for its life. It swings its tail at a lion's face.

quill

Some quills shake loose.
They sink into the lion's face.
Will the lion back off? Maybe.
Or it may flip the porcupine
over. That would mean the
end for the prickly animal.
Its soft belly is an easy target.

TAKE A LOOK!

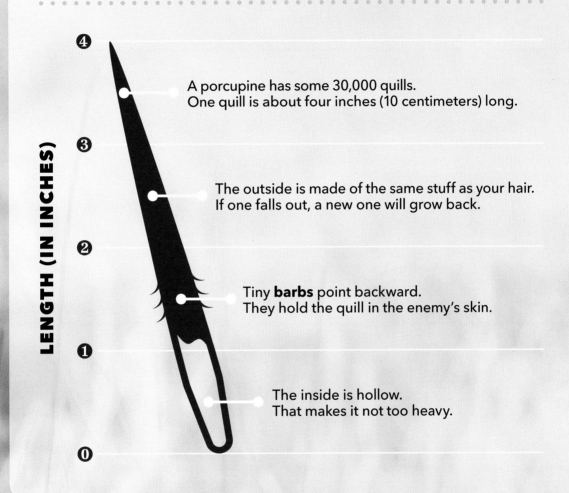

LENGTH (IN INCHES)

4 — A porcupine has some 30,000 quills. One quill is about four inches (10 centimeters) long.

3 — The outside is made of the same stuff as your hair. If one falls out, a new one will grow back.

2 — Tiny **barbs** point backward. They hold the quill in the enemy's skin.

1 — The inside is hollow. That makes it not too heavy.

0

A Chilean rose tarantula
likes to mind its own business.
This fuzzy spider can be
a lovable pet. But if you
bother it, watch out!
It kicks tiny hairs off its
body. Those hairs can stick
into your eyes. They dig
in like shards of glass.

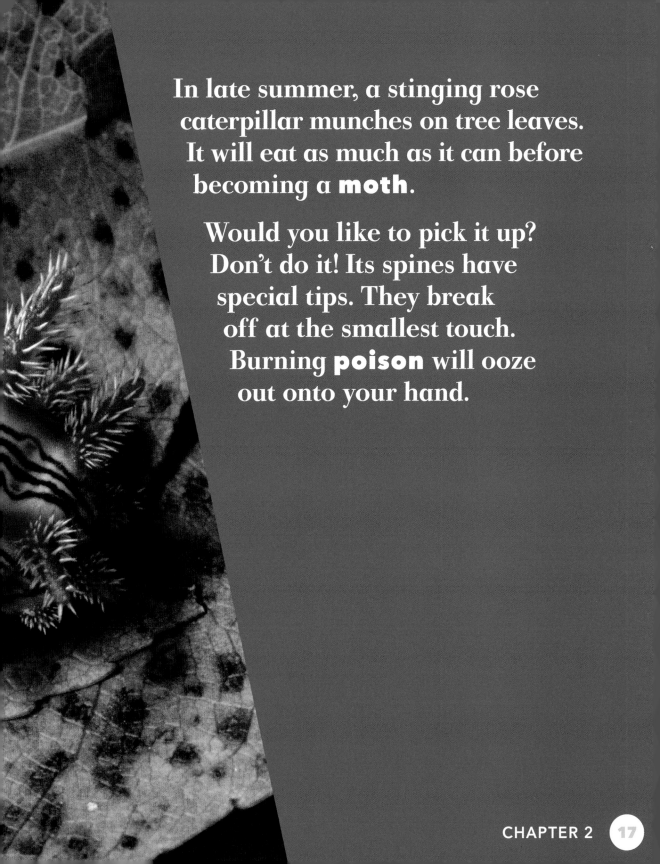

In late summer, a stinging rose caterpillar munches on tree leaves. It will eat as much as it can before becoming a **moth**.

Would you like to pick it up? Don't do it! Its spines have special tips. They break off at the smallest touch. Burning **poison** will ooze out onto your hand.

CHAPTER 3

PRICKLY SURPRISES

Some animals hide their prickles until the time is right. Most often, a blowfish looks like a regular fish.

When it senses trouble, the fish gulps up water. It blows up like a balloon. Sharp spines stick out from all sides. It doesn't look so tasty now.

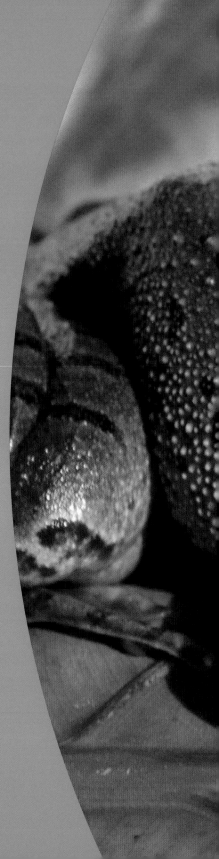

The hairy frog is known in Africa as the horror frog. Wonder why? Hunters in Africa know never to pick up this creature. If they do, the frog tenses special **muscles**. The muscles break bones in its legs. Then the bones push sharp claws out the frog's toes. Ouch!

ACTIVITIES & TOOLS

RAISE A WOOLLY BEAR CATERPILLAR

A woolly bear caterpillar's bristles keep predators away. But this fuzzy bug is safe to hold. You may find one in a garden in spring or fall. Bring it inside, and watch it turn into a tiger moth.

You will need:

- a plastic jar
- twigs
- leaves from outside
- a wooly bear caterpillar

Steps:

❶ Set up your woolly bear's house. Have an adult put some holes in the lid of your plastic jar. Throw in a mix of leaves and a twig or two.

❷ Find a woolly bear in spring or fall. Carefully pick it up. The woolly bear will curl up into a ball. It is okay.

❸ Lovingly place your pet in its new home. Add fresh leaves every day. Your woolly bear wakes up at night.

❹ Wait for your woolly bear to spin its cocoon. Your pet may become very chubby and slow. It may shed its coat and change color. Be patient, and keep watching. Clean out the jar if it looks dirty.

❺ A magical change is happening inside the cocoon. After a week or more, a tiger moth comes out. Bring it outside, and set it free!

GLOSSARY

barb: A point that sticks out backward on something sharp, such as a fishhook. The barb makes it hard for the fishhook to fall out of the fish's mouth.

moth: A flying insect that looks a lot like a butterfly. Moths usually come out only at night.

muscle: A body part that makes animals move.

poison: Something that can make you sick when you eat it or touch it.

predator: An animal that kills other animals for food.

prey: An animal that is killed and eaten by other animals.

quill: An animal's sharp, hollow prickle.

spine: The word scientists use for any kind of prickle on an animal's body.

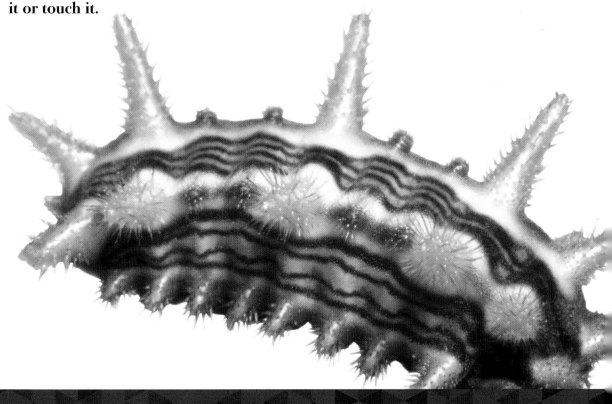

INDEX

TO LEARN MORE

Learning more is as easy as 1, 2, 3.

1) Go to www.factsurfer.com

2) Enter "pricklyanimals" into the search box.

3) Click the "Surf" button to see a list of websites.

With factsurfer, finding more information is just a click away.